PET REPAIR

Jack H. McElyea, D.V.M. with Jane Warnock McElyea

Cover Design, Calligraphy and Illustrations by
Marta Shattuck Romansky

Typesetting by Scott Richards Graphics

ISBN: 0-9615622-4-2

Printed in the United States of America by
Vaughan Press

TABLE OF CONTENTS

INTRODUCTION

Who loves me will also love my dog.
Bernard Clairboux

This book is written in simple form. A person can read through it several times and know what first aid to render in most cases without having to go back to the source. It is designed to give you information on how to choose and take care of a pet.

A bone to the dog is not charity. Charity is a bone shared with the dog when you are just as hungry as the dog.

J. London

HISTORY OF THE DOG

Dogs as well as cats descended from a common ancestor called the Meoies. This was a long headed, short legged animal that also was the ancestor of the bear, fox, weasel, and many more mammals.

The closeness between today's humans and their dogs can be accounted for by an association thought to date back about 20,000 years.

FROM THE MOUTHS OF BABES

When our son John was about three, he was thrilled that I was letting him stand on a stool to watch a Caesarean section. I cautioned him that since the female dog had been in delivery for over 24 hours, the pups might be sick or not even alive. He thought for a minute, then asked, "Daddy, if they're not alive, what will you do — put them back and let them grow some more?"

A cat's a cat and that's that!

HISTORY OF THE CAT

Cats have been associated with man for about 5,000 years.

Cats domestication was accomplished by the Egyptians, who worshipped them. Some of the Egyptian rulers insisted their cats be buried with them. Poor Cats!

SLOW DOWN, KITTY!

A mother and son were sitting in the reception room of the veterinarian waiting to get their cat neutered. The little boy wanted the operation described.

The mother said the vet was going to fix him so he wouldn't chase girl cats anymore. The son replied, "What are they going to do, fix him so he can't run?"

OLD PETS' TALES

TALE: Scooting on his bottom means your pet has worms.

TRUTH: Scooting means an itchy bottom — of which tape worms are an infrequent cause. Treatment is to clean with water and apply white vaseline to rectal area.

TALE: Hot nose means fever. Moist, cold nose means good health.

TRUTH: Cold, moist, or hot nose only means your pet is, or is not, sweating.

TALE: Rabies occurs more frequently during "dog days" - the months of July, August and early September.

TRUTH: Rabies is equally dangerous and prevalent year round.

All animals are equal, but some animals are more equal than others.

Animal Farm (1945) Chapter 10
George Orwell

YOUR VETERINARIAN

Never a dull cat.

CHOOSING YOUR PET'S VETERINARIAN

Other than you and your family, your pet's best friends are your veterinarian and his staff.

The best time to visit your veterinarian with a new pet is the same time he joins your family — even on the way home from his acquisition.

When you arrive in a new town or city, one of the first things to do is select your new place of worship and then locate the veterinarian.

Unless there is a good reason, choose the doctor nearest where you live. If you don't like him, ask friends and/or neighbors which veterinarian they use.

HOW TO HELP YOUR VETERINARIAN HELP YOUR PET

1. Before your office visit, write down your pet's medical history. Bring it to your appointment.
2. Provide a stool specimen for an internal parasite examination on each visit.
3. Call and report on your pet's health progress when your veterinarian makes this request.

4. Make your telephone conversation brief and concise.
5. Follow your veterinarian's instructions on treatment and pet care to the best of your ability.

SHOT DOWN!

One of our good friends brought her beagle in for his vaccinations. The friend was in a big, big hurry. As she watched me go from one examination room to the next, she very nicely said, "Please hurry. I'm in a time crunch." I replied, "I will, just as soon as I get to your dog."

One reason why a dog is such a lovable creature is that his tail wags instead of his tongue.

CHOOSING A PUPPY OR KITTEN FOR YOUR FAMILY

Happiness is the scent of a puppy's breath.

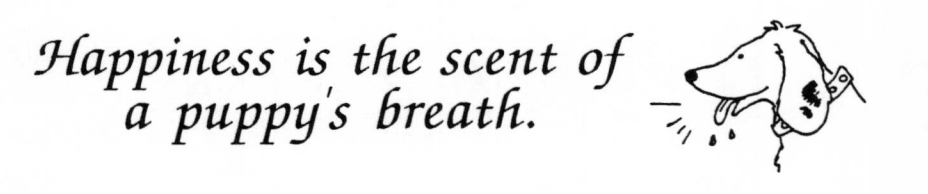

1. Choose a kitten or puppy that is out-going, one that will come to you and shows love and affection.
2. Do not select a puppy or kitten with body sores or lesions, no matter what the cause.

3. If choosing from a litter, it is easy to sit down with them and select the one with the most out-going personality.
4. Choose a puppy with full knowledge of how big he will be when grown.

THE BAKING OF THE PUPS STORY

Late one night, I was called to the clinic to perform a Caesarean section. When I delivered the puppies, they were weak and cold. I brought them home, put them on a cookie sheet and turned on the oven to warm them. Then I placed the puppies inside, using the oven as an incubator.

I was up so late attending to the puppies' needs that my wife got up to see what was going on. When she asked what I was doing, I said baking puppies. Giving me a strange look, she rushed over to the oven to see for herself — and it was really true!

DISCIPLINE AND REWARD

*A dog teaches a boy fidelity,
perserverance and to turn around
three times before sitting down!*
Robert Benchley

DISCIPLINE

Very little punishment is needed, and the punishment should never be severe. A scolding, a slight tap with a folded newspaper, or a clap of the hands will get your pet's attention when he is doing something wrong.

REWARD

The best way to reward your pet is to give him a Brewer's Yeast tablet. Make it a game. Shake the bottle of tablets several times before you reward him with a tablet or two.

The one thing that money can't buy,
the wag of a dog's tail.

Josh Billings

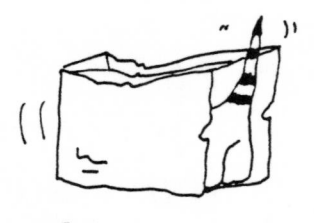

*There's nothing cuter than a kitten,
a tennis ball and a large empty
brown grocery bag.*

HOUSE TRAINING

Kittens are self house-breaking if a litter box is provided. If you have any trouble with the litter you are using, try builder's sand.

Puppies are a little more difficult — sometimes impossible! Take your puppy to the same place in the yard each time you take him out. As soon as he performs, carry him back into the house and reward him.

Important times for these outings are:
- First thing in the morning
- After each feeding
- When coming home, no matter how short the absence
- Before going to bed

Take any mistakes to that same place in the yard to give the area that distinctive odor.

A playpen for a small pup gives him the security he needs. It also prevents accidents while you are house-breaking them. Any farm or feed store can make a welded wire playpen that measures four feet square by four feet high. This can be used in the house or in the yard.

P.S. Baby playpens work great, too!

SANITATION

In a cat's eyes, all things belong to the cat!

SANITATION FOR YARD

Pick up droppings and place them in a garbage can. Washing them into the ground is simply planting the worm eggs contained in the droppings for future growth.

HOUSE-CLEANING AFTER YOUR PET'S MISTAKE

URINE: Blot dry thoroughly with tissue. After this procedure, pour a little club soda on the soiled spot and blot dry again with tissue.

FECAL MATERIAL: Pick up as best you can, then rub thoroughly with corn meal. Now vacuum. After vacuuming, clean with club soda. Blot dry with paper towels or tissue.

I am his highness' dog at kew: Pray tell me Sir, whose dog are you?

Alexander Pope

FEEDING

*How we animals differ in the
ways we do things!
Take a cat.
It laps milk with the underside
of it's tongue.
You try it!*

Feeding a pet may vary greatly. Your veterinarian can advise you on this.

The person who feeds the pet will be the star of his life and will be loved more by the pet than other members of the family.

Veterinarians go to the dogs.

EXERCISE

*The more people I meet,
the more I like my dog.*

Exercise is very important in dogs of all ages. It is crucial in the first six months of life in large breeds.

The longer the older dog exercises, the longer he will feel like exercising.

A dog is the only thing on this earth that loves you more than he loves himself. Josh Billings

TRAVELING WITH YOUR PET

Webster's definition of a pet:
An animal that is tamed or
domesticated and kept as a favorite
or treated with affection.

GENERAL

When traveling with your pet, be sure not to overfeed him. Give him a less bulky meal than he normally enjoys and restrict his water intake. It is better to take your pet's water from home than to depend on water that might taste strange to him.

Always take your rabies vaccination certificate with you when traveling with your pet.

DOGS, especially small dogs, should wear a "Figure 8" harness and be on a leash at all times when being walked in a strange place. It is easier to control large dogs and even possible to pick up a small dog if necessary with a Figure 8 harness.

Anytime a cat or dog is around water or a boat dock, he should wear a Figure 8 harness. If your pet should fall into the water, this is the only kind of harness that you can pick them up with on a boat hook.

CATS travel better in a well ventilated, dark box that protects them from road noise.

AUTOMOBILE

NEVER, NEVER LEAVE YOUR PET ALONE IN A PARKED OR STANDING CAR — NO MATTER HOW SHORT THE TIME!!!
I have seen a number of distraught pet owners from this totally avoidable accident.

NEVER, EVER LEAVE YOUR PET ALONE IN A PARKED CAR WITH THE AIR-CONDITIONING ON!

If the motor stalls, the air conditioning becomes a heater within minutes, thus causing severe, sometimes fatal, heat prostration.

TRAVELING BY COMMERCIAL CARRIER

A person owns a dog.
A cat owns the person.

WITHIN THE UNITED STATES AND CANADA

If shipping your pet by plane, check with the Airline on the Federal Temperature Regulations at the origin, destination and any transfer point. You could possibly arrive at the terminal and find that you can't ship your pet if the temperature is above or below Federal standards at any of the above three points.

This law might create a situation where you arrive at a certain destination with no problem, but could not leave two weeks later.

It is also a Federal regulation that you have food and water in your pet carrier.

States universally require that an animal must be vaccinated against rabies and must be accompanied by a health certificate from a federally accredited veterinarian.

OUTSIDE THE UNITED STATES

If you are planning to travel to any foreign country, you need to obtain specific instructions from your veterinarian. Frequently, certain countries have regulations that require 30-day prior planning before entering their country.

A few countries have prohibitive pet quarantine regulations.

TALE OF THE TAIL

Why do dogs always sniff each other upon their first meeting? Well, early in dog history, all the dogs were having a big party. It was the custom of the day for each dog to hang up its tail, much like humans hang up their hats when they enter a building.

Continued . . .

It seems that during this big party, the building caught fire. The dogs rushed out in such haste that they grabbed any old tail. They've been looking for their own tail ever since.

FLEA CONTROL

A dog is a heartbeat at my feet.

Edith Wharton

Fleas are an environmental problem. For every flea on your animal, there are 100 fleas in the surrounding environment.

An old saying is that an air-conditioned house with wall to wall carpeting is a climate controlled flea farm — with your pet as the feed pan.

YARD

Spray sandy, shady places each week with Malathion, or any approved insecticide.

HOUSE
(This is most important!)
1. Vacuum the house.
2. Turn all chair cushions on their sides.
3. Fog or spray the house with a product containing an insecticide for adult fleas and a larvacide (Precore) for immature fleas.

4. Don't vacuum your rugs for a week.
5. Repeat this house-spray treatment every two weeks until no fleas are seen on your pet.
6. Continue to spray your house with Precore, diluted with water only, each month whether you see fleas on your pet or not.

7. If fleas reappear on your pet, repeat the whole-house insecticide treatment again. This system will work!

   REMEMBER: Fleas on your pet mean fleas in your pet's environment.

PET

At the same time you are treating your house for fleas, treat your pet with flea powder. Never use any flea powder or insecticide on cats, kittens, or puppies that doesn't *specifically state* that it is *safe* for them.

The best method of applying flea powder to your pet is by rubbing the powder into the coat thoroughly and down into the skin. The best applicator is a dry wash cloth.

HOW BIG IS BIG?

Some friends of ours fed their beagles in immense feed pans. The only problem with this was that it scared off delivery men. The delivery men thought they had a dog in the yard large enough to go with the huge feed pans!

A good neighbor is one who hears his own dog barking!

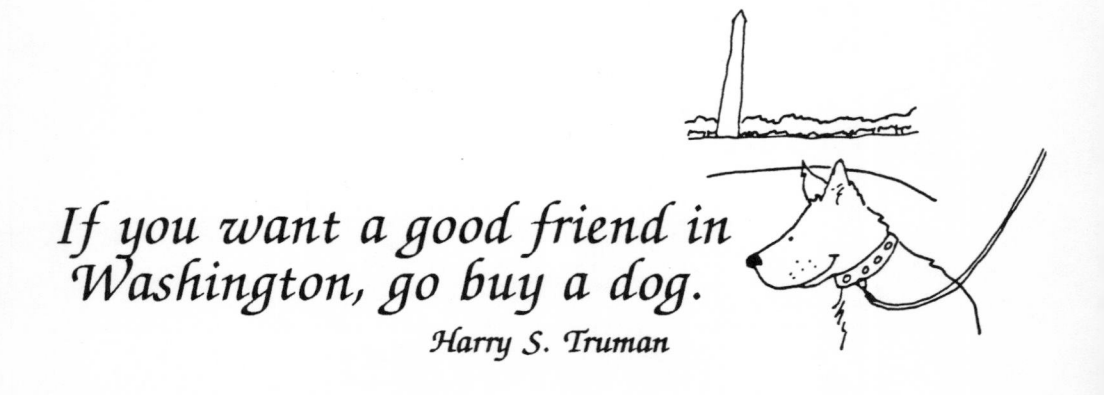

If you want a good friend in Washington, go buy a dog.

Harry S. Truman

GROOMING

Baths are not always needed for health reasons, but are needed for social reasons!

Before bathing, place a small amount of white vaseline in your pet's eyes to protect them from soap burn.

Brushing and combing your pet is very important to ensure a pretty hair coat. Cats especially should be brushed as kittens to get them used to being brushed.

Equal parts of corn starch and baby powder, brushed in and out of your pet's hair, makes an excellent dry bath.

If a cat or dog gets into heavy oil or grease, rub them with a mechanic's waterless hand cleanser. Let this cleanser stay on the animal for at least five minutes. The next step is to literally soak it off with clear water. Repeat this procedure until all the oil is off.

POODLE GROOMING

A poodle owner took her friend's poodle that badly needed to be clipped to the groomer, along with her dog. When she picked up the two poodles, she saw that her friend's dog had a gold star by his name.

The woman was very indignant and questioned why Yum Yum got a star on his *first* visit, while her dog, Beau, came in every two weeks and had never received a gold star.

Continued...

The owner of the poodle parlor stated good humoredly, "No, Beau hasn't gotten one of our gold stars, and if Yum Yum gets three gold stars, we won't groom him anymore!"

DID YOU GET THE RIGHT SHADE OF NAIL POLISH?

PARASITES

If you pick up a starving dog and make him prosperous, he will not bite you. This is the principal difference between a man and his dog.

Mark Twain

It's really a good idea to start your pet, at an early age, on an effective internal parasite control. This program will be recommended to you by your veterinarian, based on your particular geographic location.

*A home without a pet
is just a house.*

VACCINATIONS

Disease control through vaccinations is absolutely essential.

Follow the advice of your veterinarian explicitly because vaccination programs vary depending on your geographic location.

Many times I've heard pet owners state that they don't vaccinate their pet because they're never out of the house. It's better to be safe than sorry. Your pet might get exposed by a visiting friend's pet or some other unexpected turn of events.

Cat : An example of sophistication minus civilization. *Anonymous*

A kitten is so flexible that she's almost double: The hind parts are equivalent to another kitten with which the forepart plays. She does not discover that her tail belongs to her until you tread upon it.

Henry Thoreau

It is terrible to have a pet injured, but it is even worse to let the pet severely injure you while *you* are trying to help him.

Injured dogs should have their mouth tied closed before you take him to the veterinary clinic. This is a very easy and kind way to protect yourself.

Large dogs that aren't mobile can be transported by using a blanket as a stretcher.

Small dogs can be picked up in a towel.

If a cat carrier is not available, injured cats should be carried in a pillow case.

FIRST AID FOR EARS

1. **Bleeding from tip of flap:** Touch bleeding part with a Q-tip that has been dipped in full strenght liquid bleach. Apply pad of one-half mini-size Kotex pad. Hold in place with a sock that has had the toe cut out. Secure with paper tape, keeping this very loose. Wrap tape around and around the head until ear is secured to head.

2. **Cleaning your pet's ears:** Don't use Q-tips. Clean the ears with a mixture of equal parts of alcohol and olive oil. Use cotton balls to wipe out ears after cleaning.

3. Hydrogen Peroxide is NOT a useful ear cleaner. Neither is full-strength alcohol.

FIRST AID FOR EYES

1. Soap burn is a very common eye problem. Flush eye with water-soaked cotton balls. Then place *White* Vaseline in eye, pull lid closed, and gently massage.

2. It is VERY IMPORTANT not to second-guess an eye condition. Early professional treatment often is the determining factor in a happy and healthy result in eye disease. Don't hesitate to call and see your veterinarian early.

FIRST AID FOR TEETH

There's not much first aid for teeth, but you ought to know these facts:

1. Playing with a puppy by pulling a sock, etc., can loosen and extract a puppy's baby teeth.

2. Baby teeth shed and are replaced
    from four months of age to nine months
    of age.

The first teeth are lost at four months and
are in the very front of the mouth. This is
a good way of determining the age and
future size of a pup of unknown ancestry.
They are about half grown when they lose
their first teeth.

3. Rubbing a dog's gums with damp gauze and three percent hydrogen peroxide twice a week will help keep gums healthy and clean.
4. Have your pup examined by a veterinarian at five months and seven months for proper teeth shedding and alignment of permanent teeth.

FIRST AID FOR SKIN

There are so many skin conditions, and so many remedies, that this book couldn't hold them all. Let's just take a glancing look at the subject:

1. Wounds — Clip hair closely. Clean with hydrogen peroxide and discern if professional help is needed.

2. Itch — Rub with corn starch or baby powder that contains corn starch.
3. Sores — A tri-biotic ointment is a help to small skin sores or cuts.

FIRST AID FOR INSECT BITES

1. Place a small amount of baking soda on a damp cotton ball and apply to bite.
2. Now rub the bite with hydro-cortisone cream.

FIRST AID FOR NAILS

1. A common emergency is a toe nail cut too short. The first aid for this is a little liquid bleach and a Q-tip touched to the nail...and time. Remember, a little blood goes a long way, so allow time for this to heal.

2. A second common emergency is a *torn* nail. This can be treated with a band-aid until you can take your pet to your regular veterinarian.

FIRST AID FOR VOMITING

1. Allow no food, and only a small amount of water.
2. Give pet one-half teaspoon of Donnagel for each 10 pounds of body weight.

3. Administer every four to six hours.
4. Severe or prolonged vomiting should be treated professionally.

FIRST AID FOR DIARRHEA

1. Allow **no** food.
2. Provided there is no vomiting, you may allow free access to water.
3. Treat by giving one-half teaspoon of Donnagel for each 10 pounds of body weight.
4. Administer every four to six hours.

BLEEDING

Severe bleeding can seldom be controlled by using a tourniquet. It is better to apply a pressure bandage by using a sanitary pad and paper masking tape. Seek professional help immediately. The loss of blood from external bleeding will seldom be fatal if you use a bandage and proceed to your veterinarian or an emergency clinic.

ASPIRIN OR OTHER PAIN KILLERS

Dogs can safely take small amounts of aspirin or Tylenol for pain.

CATS CANNOT TAKE ANY AMOUNT OF ASPIRIN OR TYLENOL for any purpose! Even a small amount can be fatal to cats.

DOG SWALLOWS $50 BILL

A lady presented a small dog for treatment, complaining that he had eaten a $50 bill. The vet recommended a strong laxative which produced abundant diarrhea.

"Did the dog pass the $50 bill?" the vet asked.

"No! It was counterfeit!"

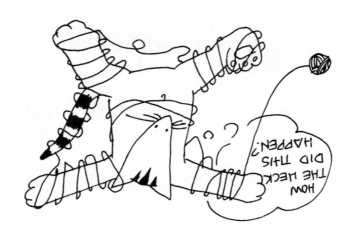

FIRST AID SUPPLIES FOR ANIMALS

These items are usually on hand in most homes:

1. Three percent (3%) Peroxide (for teeth, gums, and wounds)
2. White Vaseline (eyes)
3. Baby powder or anti-fungal foot powder (skin)

4. Alcohol and olive oil (mixed in equal parts for use in ears)
5. Burn ointment
6. Tri-biotic or neosporin ointment (wounds)
7. Hydro-cortisone cream (skin)
8. Sanitary pads (wounds)
9. Two-inch (2") masking tape or paper tape (wounds)
10. Donnagel (nonprescription drug for diarrhea and/or vomiting)

11. Veterinary clinic phone number.
12. Phone number of off-hours veterinary emergency clinic.
13. A rectal thermometer **should not be** included in your first-aid drawer — unless you have been professionally instructed on how to hold an animal when using it. A thermometer broken off and/or lost in a pet becomes a real emergency.

WHEN FIRST AID SHOULD *NOT* BE USED

Some conditions do not warrant first aid, but immediate professional emergency care. In such cases your pet should be rushed to a veterinary clinic or emergency clinic as soon as possible.

Among these conditions are:

1. Snake bite: Don't even waste time to kill the snake for indentification. Your veterinarian will know how to treat your pet according to its symptoms.

2. Poisoning of any kind: Take the pet and the poison container or plant with you to the veterinary clinic.
3. Serious accidents: Time is of the essence when there has been automobile trauma, dog fights, burns and other such accidents.
4. Drowning: If your pet falls in the swimming pool, off a seawall or boat, hurry to the clinic. This is very common in old, blind dogs.

GOOD NEIGHBOR (?)

A person presented and paid for a debarking operation that was apparently successful because several weeks later the same dog was presented for his loss of ability to bark. It seems the dog had not been able to bark since his neighbor had kept him for him to go on a family vacation! (The "good" neighbor had had his dog debarked)

POISONINGS

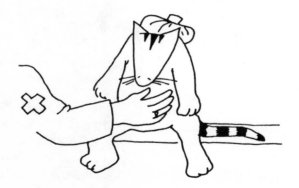

The best treatment for poisoning is prevention!!

If your pet consumes poison, however, take the pet and the poison container to your veterinarian immediately.

TIPS ON POISON PREVENTION

1. Warfarin and DeCon: Place Warfarin and DeCon rat poisoning packages in high places. Nail or screw them into a stationary board where the rats can't knock them to the floor.

2. Poison pills and powders: Put all poison pills and powders in a small-mouth jar so that bugs can get in but your pet's tongue cannot.

3. Roach hives: Take the pills out of roach hives and place them in a small-mouth bottle.
4. Auto coolant: Always place a piece of cardboard where you park your car to catch the overflow from the radiator. One teaspoon of auto anti-freeze is enough to cause irreversible kidney damage to your cat or dog, leading to death.

5. House plants: So many house plants are poisonous that we must consider them all poisonous. Keep them out of reach of all pets — especially puppies and kittens.

6. Insecticides and herbicides: Remember, if a product kills insects and/or plants, it will at least make your pet sick if over-exposed to the chemical.

EDUCATED HOUND

A city slicker listened to a hound dog chasing a fox, exclaimed what a good, clear voice the dog had. Suddenly the hound stopped baying for a few minutes, and then began again. His owner explained that the dog was so smart he didn't bark while running over posted property!

PREGNANCY AND SEX

1. The duration for pregnancy for dogs is nine weeks.
2. The duration for pregnancy for cats is eight weeks.
3. Dogs should be presented for a health examination when they are six weeks pregnant.

4. Cats should be presented for a health examination when they are five weeks pregnant.
5. Either should deliver within three hours of first signs of straining. Otherwise professional help should be sought immediately.

6. Cats seldom have trouble delivering their kittens, but when they do, professional help is needed.
7. If dogs have trouble delivering, professional help should be sought. The smaller the female, the more likelihood of delivery problems.

8. A rare need for first aid, but an important one, in puppy delivery is an uncleaned pup. If this happens, do the following:
   a. Break sack or pup envelope, the way you would peel a grape.
   b. Hold pup with head down and clean mouth and nose of mucous with a cloth towel.
   c. Tie the cord with thread one inch from pup and cut cord leaving thread with pup.

9. Male and female dogs and cats can be fertile anytime from approximately six months of age.
10. If you are fortunate, or unfortunate, enough to have a female dog that has a large litter of puppies, mark them in groups of three's by tying different colors of yarn around their necks. Taking three of one color at the time makes it easier to observe them in groups while you are feeding and caring for them.

SPAYING YOUR PET

Spaying female dogs or cats between the ages of six months to five years will lengthen their life and greatly reduce the problems of old age. For example:

- Uterus infection — 100% prevented
  Mammary tumors — Almost 100% prevented

- Freedom from accidental breeding
- Freedom from the three weeks of vaginal bleeding each six months in the dog and the freedom of owning a wild female cat each spring and fall.

CASTRATING

Castrating a male dog or cat between one year and four years will nearly always alleviate the old age problems of:

- Prostate problems
- Tumors around the rectum
- Tumors of the testicles and scrotum
- Wandering in search of a female
- Castrating also helps sometime with fighting and wall-spraying in male cats.

STORE-KEEPING DOG

Two young people were bragging to an old-timer about how smart their dog was. They said they could send their dog to the store to buy meat, and he would return with the exact change. When the old-timer was asked how smart his dog was, he replied, "Not very... but he runs that store where your dog trades."

ESPECIALLY FOR KITTENS

Keep all cabinets, dresser drawers, washing machine and clothes dryer doors closed. Keep the lid down on laundry hampers. Kittens like to cuddle up in the soft clothes and might have the door closed on them with disastrous results.

Don't forget, never give your cat aspirin, tylenol or narcotic. It can be fatal.

CONSTIPATION

Constipation symptoms in a male cat are most frequently caused by complete urinary tract blockage. Early veterinary treatment is essential. Delay in treatment of these symptoms can be fatal.

HAIR BALLS IN CATS

Hair balls can be treated with any cat laxative obtained from your veterinarian.

To help prevent hair balls, place one or two teaspoons of PURE LARD (NOT VEGETABLE OIL) in your cat's food. This lubricates their stomachs plus gives them a healthier coat, thus preventing hair loss.

The frequent brushing of your kitten with a lady's hair brush will also prevent hair from entering the stomach.

A cat in gloves catches no mice.
Ben Franklin

GOOD? MORNING!

It was 3 o'clock in the morning. The phone rang. It was answered with a sleepy hello. The voice on the other end greeted his neighbor with a cheery, "Good Morning!"

The neighbor replied, "My goodness, man, do you know it's 3 o'clock in the morning!"

The man replied, "Your dog was making so much noise, I thought it was time to get up."

BIRDS

If your dog and cat veterinarian is not a qualified Bird Doctor, he will be the first to tell you. In that case find a specialist just for your bird.

Prevention is very important in the health of birds. Here are some do's and don't's for the good health of your bird.

1. Provide a constant temperature recommended by your bird specialist for your particular breed of bird.
2. Provide a draft-free location for the bird's cage - away from air condition vents and windows.
3. Do not allow your bird out of his cage unattended.

4. Do not let your bird out of the cage in the day time. They are prone to fly into closed windows, trying to get outside.
5. Ceiling fans claim many bird casualties.

NUTRITION

Your bird needs more than bird seed. Start a young bird on a proper feeding program. Consult an expert of your particular breed who is a breeder or a veterinary specialist.

6. When taking your bird to the veterinary clinic, you can put him in a smaller cage for the trip, but take his regular cage with at least twelve hours of undisturbed fecal material in the floor of the cage. This helps with a routine examination.

7. A Q-tip dipped in full strength clorox will usually stop beak and toe-nail bleeding. **CAUTION: DO NOT HOLD A BIRD UPSIDE DOWN FOR THIS TREATMENT.** Wrap him in a small towel and hold him in the natural upright position.

THE WINNER IS...

When I go to the race track, I must always pick the best horse because it takes all the other horses running as hard as they can to beat him.

The most distraught pet owners I have seen have been the ones that have lost a pet in a closed, hot car.

The happiest clients I have seen are ones who have replaced a lost pet with a new wiggly tailed pup or frisky kitten.

Even when the bird walks, we see that it has wings.

Antoine-Marin Lemierre

Jack H. McElyea was born in Leesburg, Lake County, Florida. He moved to Webster, Sumter County, Florida when he was eight and lived there until he joined the Coast Guard in World War II. He graduated from the University of Florida with a Bachelor of Science in Agriculture and from Auburn University with a Doctorate degree in Veterinary Medicine.

He has practiced Veterinary Medicine in Orlando, Florida for the past thirty-three years.

He and his wife, Jane, have three grown children, Pam, John and Jeff and two grandsons, Paul and Brad - and one grandchild on the way!

Jane Warnock McElyea was born in Webster, Sumter County, Florida. She attended Florida Southern College in Lakeland, where she was a member of Delta Zeta sorority. She graduated from Rollins College in Winter Park, Florida.

Jane has co-authored, with daughter Pam, four best sellers: *Advice... Southern Style; Just Between You & Me...; A Toast To You... And You... and You! (A Toast For Every Occasion);* and a cookbook, *Sweet Surrender with Advice ala Carte.*

One of my husband's clients & an old family friend, wrote this portion of a poem about him. She wrote it as one pet introducing the new puppy to the family & to their veterinarian.

A P.S. , alas! How could I forget?!
Doc Mac's his name. his calling . . . our vet.
I'd love to omit this annual trip.
My stomach churns like I have the grippe.
No wonder I'm not in the best of moods;
with my nerves on edge, the tension exudes.
After just one visit, Doc knows you inside and out.
Of that you can be sure; there's no need to doubt.
People call him a vet, I think;
but just between us, he's really a shrink.
No point in planning a scheme you'll find;
he can look right at you and read your mind.

I've hissed, I've snapped and spit his pills back,
hoping against hope his cool exterior would crack.
I've even stood my fur on end,
but for nothing will he bend.
There's no use trying to give him the slip.
Believe me, I know, he has a firm grip.
Of course I always know what the outcome will be,
but my reputation's intact- cantankerous and feisty.
My mom claims that's why I'm never sick,
I'm so ornery even bad germs leave my bailiwick.
Now, Sadie, I have a secret to confide in you;
there's a reason behind all that I do.

Beware! His M.O. can be quite disarming;
if you fall for it, you'll believe him charming.
He walks into the room all wreathed in a smile
as if he's a friend, a pal, come to visit a while.
From above his glasses he peers at you,
and you're eye to eye for a moment or two.
If allowed, he'll pat you here and there
acting as though you're a compatible pair.
Then just when you think you've got it made,
into his pocket he reaches and your hopes fade.
Because at this point with needles in hand,
it's combat time in Animal Land.

I've been testing Dr. Mac, you see,
to find if he truly loves all animals that be.
And I honestly have to admit he does indeed
as he puts up with me and the life I lead.
So after all is said and done,
My mom gives him A Plus; I say he's number ONE!
It's to him we owe our fine lives and all.
He keeps us healthy, sound and standing tall.
And if some day I succumb
to one of those evil illnesses that make one glum,
I do hope Doc Mac will be there to see me through.
He's the top of the line, first class, no other will do!

Linda Hayes